PRAYERS

FOR

WORSHIP

by

PATRICIA BATSTONE

MOORLEY'S Print & Publishing

British Library Cataloguing in Publication Data.
A catalogue record for this book is available
from the British Library.

ISBN 0 86071 496 9

MOORLEY'S Print & Publishing
23 Park Rd., Ilkeston, Derbys DE7 5DA
Tel/Fax: (0115) 932 0643

INTRODUCTION

This collection of prayers is in one sense a random assortment but in another, ordered into logical groups, the first four following the Christian Calendar - though with the addition of New Year.

Part V contains prayers for a number of other special occasions common to all denominations and the selection concludes with a number of general prayers. I favour this kind of arrangement to sub-dividing by the TYPE of prayer.

Most have been used in acts of worship, from the very formal to those less formal situations such as holiday fellowships. A few have already been published and the remainder, largely the personal ones, simply ARE!

PATRICIA BATSTONE
July, 1997

CONTENTS

PART I: ADVENT TO EPIPHANY

ADVENT:

1. An Act of Praise 1
2. A Prayer of Confession 2
3. Act of Confession 2
4. Advent Candles 3
5. Prayers of Intercession for Advent and Christmas 4
6. Dedication 6
7. Closing Prayer 6
8. A Personal Prayer for Advent 7

CHRISTMAS:

9. Midnight Praise 8
10. Christmas Confession 8
11. A Child's Thanksgiving 9
12. Christmas Night Dedication 10
13. A Personal Dedication 10

NEW YEAR:

14. A Watchnight Prayer 11
15. New Year Thanksgiving 12
16. Prayer of Commitment 13
17. My New Year Prayer 13

EPIPHANY:

18. Offerings of Worship 14
19. Confession 14
20. Prayers of Intercession at Epiphany 15
21. Thanksgiving for Gifts 16
22. Dedication 17
23. Personal Epiphany 17

PART II: LENT TO PASSIONTIDE

24.   Ash Wednesday 18
25.   A Litany for Lent 18
26.   Lenten Hope 20
27.   Act of Confession 20
28.   Closing Prayer and Benediction 21
29.   Prayer for Passion Sunday 21
30.   Palm Sunday Praise 22

HOLY WEEK:

31.   Prayer for Good Friday Worship 23
32.   Litany for Good Friday 23
33.   A Good Friday Benediction 25
34.   A Personal Good Friday 25
35.   A Litany for Holy Saturday 26
36.   Renewing Our Vows 27

PART III: EASTER TO ASCENSION

EASTER DAY:

37.   Easter Praise 28
38.   Our Confession 28
39.   Prayers of Intercession for the Easter Season 29
40.   Personal Questions in the Garden 30
41.   Prayers for Good Shepherd Sunday 30
42.   A Closing Prayer 31

ASCENSION:

43.   Ascension Vision 32
44.   Petition for Ascensiontide 33
45.   Ascension Light 33

PART IV: PENTECOST TO TRINITY

PENTECOST:

46.   Praise and Confession 34
47.   A Prayer of Confession 35

v

48. Offering 35
49. Birthday Dedication 35
50. Responsive Praise 36
51. Prayers of Intercession for the Renewal of the Church 37
52. Personal Pentecost 39

TRINITY

53. Corporate Praise and Invocation 40
54. Petitionary Prayer 41
55. Trinity Praise 42
56. Praise to the One in Three 43
57. From the Beginning 44

PART V: OTHER TIMES AND SEASONS

ST LUKE'S DAY - Liturgies for Healing:

58. Healing and Reconciliation 45
59. Prayers of Confession and Intercession on the
    Theme of Healing 48
60. Prayers for Renewal and Healing 51
61. A Liturgy of Healing for People and Places 53

ONE WORLD WEEK:

62. Praise for God's World 56
63. Prayer of Confession 57

REMEMBRANCE DAY:

64. In Praise of God Who Remembers 58
65. In Perspective 59
66. Act of Confession for Remembrance Day 60
67. Prayers of Intercession for Remembrance Day 61
68. Responsive Prayers of Intercession for
    Remembrance Sunday 62
69. Personal Memories 66
70. Prayers of Confession and Intercession for
    All Saints' Day 67

MISSION:

71. A Prayer of Approach 70
72. Working Together with God:
    Prayer of Intercession on the Theme of Mission 70
73. A General Prayer 73
74. A Litany of Praise 74
75. A Prayer of Confession 75

BIBLE SUNDAY:

76. Prayers for Bible Sunday 76
77. A Bible Sunday Thanksgiving 78
78. Prayers of Confession and Intercession
    on the Theme of Unity 80

PART VI: GENERAL PRAYERS

79. A Prayer of Approach 82
80. A 'Meeting' Prayer 82
81. Praise to the Living God 83
82. A Holiday Fellowship Prayer 83
83. A Morning Prayer 84
84. Prayer before Worship 84
85. Evening Praise 85
86. Invocation 86
87. Act of Confession: The Open Book 86
88. A General Confession 87
89. A General Intercession 88
90. Prayer of Dedication 89
91. An Offertory Prayer 89
92. Prayers of Intercession: In Trust and Confidence 90

Acknowledgements

I acknowledge with gratitude the many congregations in the Methodist Circuits in which I have served as a local preacher, without whose need the majority of these prayers would never have been written. Thanks are also due to, as they were then, Methodist Guild Holidays and Holiday Hotels for opportunities to lead worship at holiday fellowship groups.

To the editors of the following publications in which some of the material used here has been published:

Worship and Preaching (The Methodist Publishing House, Peterborough): Apr/June 1988 (N°. 89*); Oct/Dec. 1991 (N°. 59); Apr/June 1994 (N°. 32); Oct/Dec. 1994 (N°. 5); July/Sept. 1996 (N°s. 48, 50, 74, 75, 79, 81, 86);

Health and Healing Bulletin, (Methodist Church Social Responsibility Division), Summer 1992 (N°. 58)
Seven Whole Days (Arthur James, Evesham) 1992 (N°s. 58 & 59)

Time and the Gospel: Poems and Meditations for the Christian Year (Cottage Books Publications, Dunkeswell, Devon) 1995 (No. 53)

To the Methodist Publishing House for permission to use extracts from **Hymns and Psalms** 773 (N° 78), 216 (N°. 74) and 213 (N°. 39).

Scripture quotations used, with permission, all rights reserved, are from **The Revised English Bible** © Oxford University Press and Cambridge University Press 1989 (No. 59, 61, 68, 72, 76);

The Revised Standard Version of the Bible, © Old Testament 1952, New Testament 1946, complete Bible 1973 by Division of Christian Education of the National Council of the Churches of Christ in the United States of America (N°s. 32, 35, 58, 72); (Verses used are within permitted word limits).

The Good News Bible, © The Bible Societies and Collins 1976 (Nos. 5, 76);

The New Revised Standard Version, Anglicized edition, © 1989, 1995 by the United States of America (N°s. 60 and 92)

* Figures in brackets refer to the numbered prayers.

All congregational responses are printed in bold type throughout.
*** denotes a pause for additional material - names of individuals, places needs, etc. or for congregational participation, as appropriate.

PRAYERS FOR WORSHIP

PART I: ADVENT TO EPIPHANY

1. An Act of Praise

RESPONSE: "Let us praise the Lord"

Let us Praise the Lord,
"Let us praise the Lord"
Giving thanks for Jesus,
The One True Light
Who comes into our world,
Into our lives,
to give illumination to the
dark places within us.

Let us Praise the Lord,
"Let us praise the Lord"
Whose life is the Light
For all people,
A glow spreading abroad
Into the world,
to bring comfort and security
to those who are lost.

Let us Praise the Lord,
"Let us praise the Lord"
The Prince of Light
Whose power pervades
The darkness of high places,
Revealing injury and wickedness,
and opens up the way of pardon
to those who repent.

Let us Praise the Lord,
"Let us praise the Lord"
Who promises peace
in a troubled world,
Who penetrates the hearts
Of hardened beings, bringing light,
Showing them the way
of reconciliation and love.

Let us Praise the Lord,
"Let us praise the Lord"
Who is here with us in this place,
Whose light is reflected
In our hearts and lives
and will not be extinguished
by mere mortality.
As we now stand reflected
in His presence
May we shine only for Him.

Let us Praise the Lord,
"Let us praise the Lord".

2. A Prayer of Confession
(based on Isaiah 59:12-14)

The word of the prophet comes to us as it came so long ago and we, too, are guilty and in need of pardon. But the wonder is that we are not beyond redemption. We have in Jesus the One Who saves us from ourselves, from our human inclinations, and holds out the hand of blessing and forgiveness.

We come quietly to voice that guilt and to express our sorrow.

We come also to hear Your wonderful word of grace:
your sins are forgiven -
and we thank You.

Amen.

3. Act of Confession

God our Father, You promise us so much if only we will trust You.

Forgive us when we have found it so difficult to trust;
when we have despaired in the face of Your promise of hope;
when we have sunk in doubt as You called us to faith;
when we have perpetuated enmity and distrust while You were speaking peace;
when we have failed to recognise the enormity of Your love for us,
Your acceptance of us, because the world rejected us;
when we have nursed our hurts and worried about our wounds instead of turning to You for healing.

Help us to make this Advent a time of renewal, a time of hope, expectancy, faith and peace in our lives, a time when we hear and accept Your voice speaking to us: "I am He Who comforts you."

Amen.

4. Advent Candles

God, You come to us in so many guises. At Advent we think of Your coming as perfect humanity, but we think, too, of Your coming into our own lives and the life of our/the church, and we look to that other Advent when You will come again in fulfilment of all Your promises to us.

We light these candles as tokens of those promises, and our gratitude for Your fulfilment of them.

Thank You for all Your people, everywhere and at all times in history, especially for those who have set supreme examples of faith by which we may be challenged and encouraged.

R. As Your people in the world today, help us to play our part in ensuring that the light of faith is always in evidence somewhere.

Thank You for the prophets, not only the ancient seers who kept alive the hope that one day Messiah would come, but the prophets of our own day, in tune with You, who direct our way and show us the implications of our actions.

R. As Your servants, help us to listen to and discern Your message for the world today.

Thank You for John the Baptist who paved the way and prepared people for Your coming.

R. As Your witnesses, help us to follow in his footsteps, continually clearing the way for Your coming into new hearts.

Thank You for Mary, she who asked nothing of You yet was asked to give all of her being to be used by You in Your great saving work.

R. As your followers, help us to be as willing and obedient to Your call as Mary was, for our task will never be so hard, nor our response so great.

And thank You for Jesus, who came as a Light to the world, bread to the hungry, water to the thirsty, and who opened up the way to eternity and revealed Your truth, offering everlasting life to all who forgot themselves in seeking You.

R. As Your children, we pray that we may radiate the Light of Christ in all that we say and do and are. **Amen.**

5. Prayers of Intercession for Advent and Christmas

Response: **And grant the Peace of Your Presence**

The Lord promises in the last days, *"Now I make all thing new... I am the first and the last, the beginning and the end."* *(Revelation 21:5,6)*

To Him Who is Alpha and Omega, the First and the Last, we bring our prayers at this Christmas season, seeking closer communion with Him and with all His people.

V. Lord, grant us the knowledge of Your communion with us now.
R. And grant the Peace of Your Presence.

'The Lord said, "Sing for joy... I am coming to live among you." At that time many nations will come to the Lord and become His people.'
(Zechariah 2:10-11)

We pray for the nations of the world and their leaders. For some nations, politically this has been a turbulent year. For many it has brought peace and freedom, for others the sound and sight of warfare. We ask that the traditional Christmas truce from hostility may permeate the hearts of oppressed and oppressor that together they might seek peace, not war, and that hatred among nations and people might be put at an end.

V. Lord, may love and not hatred come into Your world.
R. And grant the Peace of Your Presence.

The angel of the Lord appeared to Joseph and foretold the birth of Jesus: *"He will be called Immanuel" (which means "God is with us")*
(Matthew 1:23).

But at His nativity there was no room for Him to be born - no one wanted Him.

We remember in our prayers today people throughout the world who are homeless, and destitute, children who are unwanted, victims of war and famine, of the inhumanity of those who have power of word or weapon.

V. Lord, may those who have much have compassion on those in need.
R. And grant the Peace of Your Presence.

Jesus came into the world and left us with the great commission, *"Go...*
to all people everywhere and make them My disciples... in the Name of the
Father, the Son and the Holy Spirit... and I will be with You always to the end
of the age." *(Matthew 29:20)*

We pray for those who are called to spread the Gospel of Christ's Love
in the world, through practical, pastoral or prayerful means - those who
work in the ministries of healing and of caring, of evangelism, of
spreading God's Word by all means, that the Word made Flesh in Jesus
might come and dwell in the hearts of people everywhere.

V. Lord, grant all who work and pray with You the power of Your
Spirit.
R. And grant the Peace of Your Presence.

"A large crowd of people... had come to hear Him and to be healed of their
diseases... for power was going out from Him and healing them all."
(Luke 6:17, 19)

We pray for those who are sick, in body, mind or spirit; for the sad and
lonely, those who are rejected, persecuted for faith or principle, those
who face difficult decisions, an uncertain future; families and friends
whose relationships have broken down; those who have been bereaved
and for whom Christmas is a time of greatest hurt.

We remember especially those whom we know and love...

V. Lord, be to them healing and blessing, according to their need.
R. And grant the Peace of Your Presence.

"So then, confess Your sins to one another and pray for one another, so that
you will be healed. The prayer of a good man has a powerful effect."
(James 5:16)

During the season of peace and goodwill, may we live not to ourselves
but for others. May there always be room in our lives and hearts for
one more in need. To that end we commit ourselves to becoming, as
far as in us lies, the answer to our prayers, in the knowledge, love and
abiding presence of our Lord Jesus Christ, and for His greater glory
here on earth. Amen.

6. Dedication

Lord Jesus, as we wait in expectation for Your coming again into the world, come anew into our hearts and lives, strengthen and renew us, and fill us with love for You and all people.

Amen

7. Closing Prayer

Father God,
   thank You for revealing Yourself through Your Son and making life possible for us.

We thank You that you reveal Yourself through Him by whatever Name we understand -
He is <u>Brother</u>, <u>Companion</u>, <u>Guide</u> to the lonely.
He is the <u>Son</u>, the Baby of Bethlehem, to the childless,
<u>Emmanuel</u> to those in need of companionship,
<u>Light</u> to the lost,
<u>Bread</u> to the hungry,
<u>Messiah</u> to the valiant,
<u>Prince of Peace</u> to the victims of war,
<u>Mighty God</u> to the downtrodden,
<u>Shepherd</u> to the wanderer,
<u>Master</u> to the servant,
<u>Servant</u> to the humblest,
<u>The Living Word of Love in all our lives,</u>
And for this we thank You

Amen

8. A Personal Prayer for Advent

Lord, Christmas is so predictable, yet each year there is a new sense of anticipation, of hope. I know exactly what's going to happen. I have the whole of this waiting time mapped out, working to a time schedule, predicting who'll send the first card, ordering my own lists, booking dates, looking forward to the climax - Christmas Eve Communion; looking back at other Christmases, other Communions, knowing that in reality the hope is so much more attractive than the aftermath with its memories and misgivings, regrets and disappointments.

Lord, let there always be Advent Hope in my heart. Let me always believe in Christmas - and in You, especially You. Amen.

CHRISTMAS

9. Midnight Praise

As the bells of the earth are ringing so we welcome You,
dear Lord, born anew into our alien, uninviting world,
reborn into our hearts and lives.

We praise You for Your goodness, Lord,
in sending us this gift - Your Son,
come to earth to reflect Your glory,
the glory of Incarnation,
In the light of which we stand today.

Father, may Your radiance stand among us,
Even as it filled the Bethlehem stable,
as it captured and shone in the lives of those poor shepherds
and gave them new hope and purpose in their lives.

As we welcome this day and all it means to humanity, renew our
hope in You.   Amen

❖ ❖ ❖ ❖ ❖

10. Christmas Confession

This Christmas, let us reflect:
                    Jesus came to bring us life,
                    to renew our hope,
                    to show us the way to the Father.

We confess that we have not always lived out that hope in our daily
lives, that we have not always reflected Your life in ours, and that we
have often gone our way, not God's.

Forgive us our failure to live up to Your intention.

We confess that, though Your Light shines on, we have so often lost our
way because we have turned off the road to contemplate other
attractions.

Forgive us our digressions and enable us to stay in the Light.

We confess that our lives do not always reflect Your Life, that we too easily fall out of step with truth and love and justice.

Forgive us our lack of love and care for others, our short-comings in our relationships and our lack of discernment and readiness to fall in with the spirit of the age.

This Christmas, as Love and Truth shine in the face of the Christ-child, wherever He is found, may we be assured of His love and peace in our hearts, of His acceptance and forgiveness; and so may we celebrate not only His coming to earth so long ago, but His coming afresh in our hearts today.

11. A Child's Thanksgiving

Thank You, Lord Jesus, for Christmas Day,
for the presents and parties,
for food and for fun.

Thank You, Lord Jesus, for coming to stay
right here in my home
with my family.

Thank You, Lord Jesus, that I can play
with my friends and our pets
in my home or theirs.

Thank You, Lord Jesus, but also I pray
for those who have nothing,
no home, toys - or love.

When I think of them, Lord, make me do every day
something for others, to give them a smile
so that they understand Christmas, too.

Amen.

12. Christmas Night Dedication

We have shared Your day, Lord.
Now may we share Your night.
May we never forget, as we commit ourselves to You again,
that life contains not only pleasure but pain.
Grant us readiness to accept both pain and pleasure
in serving and loving You.

Amen

❖ ❖ ❖ ❖ ❖

13. A Personal Dedication

At the end of this day, Lord
come to my heart;
be near to me while sleeping,
grant me Your peace for tonight,
strength for tomorrow
And hope in the years to come.

Amen

❖ ❖ ❖ ❖ ❖

NEW YEAR

14. A Watchnight Prayer

Hovering on the brink of the new year,
we look back with mixed feelings -

glad that we have reached this moment in time
which signifies another year of life, past, completed, fulfilled;
sad, that we take with us memories of those from whom we were parted;
angry at those times when we were taken for granted or misled;
hurt by the mistakes of ourselves and others, at irrevocable situations,
at harm we may have done,
knowing how much was left undone;

and apprehensive at the unknown future, viewed in the shadow of the past;
questioning our purpose in it, whether we shall see it through, what
will be our lot in terms of pain or suffering,
wondering who will stand with us on the brink of the next new year,
and whether this will be the year we succeed - or finally fail,
all the time knowing that we can only go forward and not back, that
we must live in future faith not on past failure.

We pray that we may live out this future year, learning the lessons of
the past, that our resolution to do so will be realistic and our courage
and commitment unfailing, through the strength which You alone can give.

Amen.

15. New Year Thanksgiving

Lord, it is good to be here,
in Your house of prayer;
it is with a sense of wonder
that we reflect on the changes and chances
of the year gone by,
to see Your hand at work in creation,
and in the mystery of life as it is
revealed to us.

We come in thanksgiving,
We come in reverence, awe and wonder;
We come praising,
remembering the moments when we knew You were there,
the times of depression,
the times of healing;
the times of alienation;
and those of fellowship,
the times of doubt and despair,
and those wonderful moments
when faith was renewed,
when there was light on the mountains
and a song in our hearts,
and we could join with Mary and cry,
"Tell out, my soul, the glory of the Lord."

Enhance our worship, we pray,
that every word might speak Your love,
every thought and action
demonstrate your nearness
and our willingness to be changed
into what You want us to be,
that those who meet us may see Your glory
reflected in us,
and praise You, too.

❖ ❖ ❖ ❖ ❖

16. Prayer of Commitment

Lord God, on the threshold of another year,
we commit it to You.
Be with us all at our times of most need,
meet us on our journey,
and send us on our way renewed
with Your love and power,
rejoicing in hope,
giving of ourselves in service to You
through others,
willing to be changed by You
and become more like You each day.

Amen

❖ ❖ ❖ ❖ ❖

17. My New Year Prayer

Father God, I do not know what the future holds, where I shall go, or how I shall find the way except You take my hand and lead me.

I only ask that You will be with me, that I shall know and feel Your presence and that I shall walk in Your will, no matter how difficult the way, how rough the elements, how painful the progress or how hurtful the obstacles that lay in my path.

I give this year to You. It is Yours. I am Yours. Do with me what and when and where You will.

Amen.

EPIPHANY

18. Offerings of Worship

As wise men came and brought You gifts so we come now to place before You these offerings of our worship.

Here is the gift of praise - upon our lips and in our hearts.

Here is the gift of adoration - we hold you closely in our hearts.

And here is the gift of thanksgiving - our love and gratitude.

And with these gifts we bring You, Lord, a fourth which holds them all together,

the gift of self - our lives, our prayers, our hearts, and hands held high in honour of Your Name - the Name we praise and worship, the Name we magnify today.

Amen.

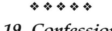

19. Confession

Lord, we remember -

We remember the times when we talked, full of excitement, never thinking of the consequences of our enthusiasm;

the times we laughed at impossibilities,
the times we drew our own conclusions, got our sums wrong, lost our way.

Lord, we are not as wise as those kings of old,
yet we see they made mistakes,
for they were human, as we are.

Lord, forgive these mistakes, our careless errors, lack of sensitivity and patience.

Forgive us when, unlike those wise men, we have not heeded Your warning voice but have allowed our own desires to obstruct Your guidance.

Lord, we thank You that You in Your infinite love and wisdom will always stay faithful to us, even when we are unfaithful to You.

Amen.

20. Prayers of Intercession at Epiphany

"Wise men came from the East to worship..."

We pray for those areas of need and the people to whom Jesus has not yet been revealed. Many are in dire need of food and shelter in the wake of famine and war but so often these desperate circumstances make them aware of their spiritual needs.

"We pray that, like the wise men, they, too, may seek and find Jesus and desire to worship Him.

They sought this new-born King in the city and the grandeur of Herod's palace.

So many people in the world, and especially in our own society, are seeking spiritual satisfaction in the bright lights of the cities, looking to false leaders, following bad examples.

We pray that, like the wise men, they will be warned before it is too late to save them from the consequences of their mistakes.

The wise men continued to follow the Star.

Stars have become one of the cults of the age, new and yet as old as antiquity - but they need careful discernment if people are to be saved from misusing their insights.

We pray that those desperate for guidance will look to the Light of the World and not to the interpretation of galaxies.

When they found Jesus they were overjoyed.

Christianity is a religion of hope, founded on trust in a solid, reliable Saviour, yet so many servants of the Church are weighed down by responsibilities, and people see them and look away in disinterest.

We pray for ourselves as Christians and church members, that we may look, not to the preservation of buildings and the outer trappings of faith, but to the real mission of the Church, the spreading, by word and deed, of what Wesley called 'Scriptural holiness.'

They opened up their treasure chest and gave Him gifts.

The Church has a reputation for begging but as long as there is need in the world, appeals to meet those needs will go on.

We pray that we and all other like-minded people may always be willing to give to the utmost, not costing it out, but simply giving, willingly and generously, to all in need of help, trusting in God to lead us through the maze of life and opening up the way for us to receive gifts from Him.

And so they returned home another way.

So many people today have no homes, no roots, sometimes no family or even country.

We pray that as they seek new routes to acceptance, as they try to find a place on the crowded road to freedom - whether it be in becoming self-supportive, in having work and often responsibility, or in having the freedom to choose the way forward, they may be led by You.

Amen.

21. Thanksgiving for Gifts

Lord God, thank You for Your many gifts:
the kind that come through others remembering us;
the abundance of material gifts You have created,
and the even greater store of spiritual gifts.
Most of all, this is a season for giving thanks for the
greatest gift of all -

Jesus Christ our Lord.

Amen.

22. Dedication

Jesus Christ, King of kings and Lord of lords,
we give You our allegiance,
We bring You our gifts.
use us and them to Your glory, we pray.

Amen.

❖ ❖ ❖ ❖ ❖

23. Personal Epiphany

Epiphany - revelation - God showing Himself to people of another faith. It is a challenge to be savoured, meditated upon, and not to be taken lightly.

Help me, Lord, to remember that I am only one individual in a very large whole which contains millions of other individuals, not one of us alike.

And we each set out on the journey, bearing our gifts, and no two gifts are alike.

And when we have found You and offered that gift, You have a different word for each one of us, but You also encourage us to be one whole - one with You, in You and for You - for together we shall make a big difference.

❖ ❖ ❖ ❖ ❖

24. Ash Wednesday

"Ashes to ashes..."

The palm crosses have turned to ash,
ash on my fingers, ash on my forehead.
This is the season of remorse, of repentance,
of a fresh self-giving.

Lord, I come, just as I am,
bowed with the burden of my own inadequacies,
burdened with the needs of a faithless world,
needing to spend time alone - with You.

And I shall go out, out into the world,
bearing the mark of penitence,
a cross of ashes on my forehead:
the message to the world -
"It was for you..."

It was for me, too.

25. A Litany for Lent

Lent is a time for self-examination, for placing ourselves under the shadow of the Cross and seeing where we fall short in our commitment to the Lord Who died there for our sakes.

Let us look at our lives and service and confess that we have not given a fraction of what He has done for us.

Lord, we confess that we have not served You enough.

Let us consider our witness, the impression others have gained about Christianity from our example.

Lord, we confess that we have fallen short in our witness to You and that the way we live may even have turned someone away.

Let us look at our relationship with others, our reactions to the people who hurt us, our interaction with those who think and act in ways we cannot accept.

Lord, forgive us for the times when we have been unforgiving, when we have turned from holding out the hand of friendship and reconciliation.

Let us look at our church. We have often found fault with it and with those in office, yet have done nothing positive to further its witness.

Lord, forgive us for our lack of commitment to the Church, Your Body here on earth.

Let us look at the wider church community, and consider what we have done to further its united witness.

Lord, forgive us for our petty prejudices, for being judgmental and aloof.

Let us see our part in the community in which we live and ask whether we have fulfilled our commission to reach out to others with the offer of salvation.

Lord, forgive us the times when we have not worked with others for the common good and have not made You known when opportunities arose.

Let us look out on to the wider world in which we live, and ask ourselves what kind of stewards we are of the earth's resources.

Lord, forgive us when we have wilfully squandered Your gifts of nature. Help us to treasure, respect and conserve all that is most precious.

Let us look for peace in a war-torn world, and confess how little we have done to bring peace about.

Lord, forgive us when we have not prayed enough, when our hearts have been full of conflict instead of the search for peace, when our own disinterestedness has undermined the need for peace.

Finally, let us remember that we are fit and well and have plenty while others starve or die of diseases that peace could have prevented.

Father, we acknowledge our poverty of spirit in the face of others' material poverty, our richness in health and wealth in the face of the spiritual riches of those who have so little of this world's goods.

Let us look for peace in a war-torn world, and confess how little we have done to bring peace about.

Lord, hear us.

Father, hear us

We hear the Word of Grace: our sins are forgiven.

Thanks be to God.   Amen

26. Lenten Hope

Father, giver of Light and power,
We praise You;
Jesus, Light of the World,
we acknowledge You:
Holy Spirit, presence of God within us,
we open our hearts to receive You.
Triune God, Father, Son and Spirit,
perpetual Light, illuminating our lives,
we praise You, we thank You,
even as we share in the harsh realities of
the world about us,
for resurrection hope that overcomes
everything
and renews our whole lives,
mind and heart,
to the glory of Your Name,
now and always.
Amen.

❖ ❖ ❖ ❖ ❖

√ 27. Act of Confession

Father God,
There are many times
when we are blind and do not see,
when we see and do not believe,
when we are deaf and do not hear,
when we hear and do not respond.
We permit doubts to cloud our vision,
and fear to block our ears;
we are too ready to let the cares and
concerns of the world
come between us and
Your will for our lives,
Your peace in our hearts.
Father, forgive us, we pray,
and so illuminate our vision
that we may go forward in faith, believing.

Amen.

28. Closing Prayer and Benediction

Lighten the darkness of our inward vision, Lord,
And let the pure light of Your truth so
pervade our hearts and minds,
that we may discern what is good and right
and what is Your will for our lives.

Then may the Grace, Peace and Blessing
of God our Father,
through Jesus Christ the Son
and the Indwelling Holy Spirit
Be ours for ever.

Amen.

29. Prayer for Passion Sunday

Make us steadfast in Your service, Lord, and may our own lives be
an example to others of Your love for everyone. We ask it through
Him who set His face towards Calvary - Jesus Christ our Lord.

❖ ❖ ❖ ❖ ❖

30. Palm Sunday Praise

Glorious Messiah, they hailed You a King,
they crowded on to the streets,
shouting and singing and waving their palms.
They rejoiced at Your coming, proclaimed You their Saviour,
Their longed-for Redeemer, their Prince and their Lord.
And You rode in peace on that memorable day,
on a sure-footed donkey undeterred by the crowds
and the noise and the hullabaloo.

They didn't know, could not have foreseen
how soon they would change to a vicious attack
and call for Your blood, Your death on a cross...

Lord, this day we praise You, but we have in mind
the cruel events that followed that week,
and because of the scourging, the trial and the nails
we go on praising and thanking that wonderful love
that came to earth as a man to die
and raises us with You, to glory always.

HOLY WEEK

31. Prayer for Good Friday Worship

Father God, we come to praise You on what is a solemn day, the day we can only remember with shame because of the part we have retrospectively played in it, and of regret that there was no other way to save humanity from its own sinfulness, and of sadness because so many remain unable or unwilling to be saved.

As we have followed the course of the Passion we have witnessed how changeable human nature can be, how selfish and cruel. We may have shared in that fatal Eucharist, witnessed the agony of Jesus in Gethsemane, but we could not share more than a hint of it. Now we identify with the fearful disciples, the remorseful Judas, and we catch a glimpse of loneliness and dereliction.

The disciples did not see the hope that we see, could not see beyond the cruel nails and crown of thorns to a glory beyond.

We are sustained by that hope, but Father, may we never forget the cost.

In this hour we come penitently, but we come to learn. May we leave this service today strong in the knowledge that death was indeed overcome, and confident in Your abiding, loving and forgiving presence with us. Amen

32. Litany for Good Friday

"... Far be it from me to glory except in the cross of our Lord Jesus Christ, by which the world has been crucified to me, and I to the world."
(Galatians 6:14, RSV)

This is the day when we remember in penitence the innocent Jesus condemned to die while a guilty man went free.

V. He gave His life for all.
R. He gave His life for me

This is the day when we think of Jesus scourged and beaten, taking the punishment He did not deserve.

V. He gave His life for all.
R. He gave His life for me

This is the day when we recall how Jesus shouldered His cross and stumbled through the city with a burden greater almost than He could bear.

V. He gave His life for all.
R. He gave His life for me

This is the day when we listen with gratitude to the stories of those who helped Jesus on His way. We think of the women, including the one we know as Veronica who wiped His face with her scarf. We think of the man, Simon of Cyrene, whose life was changed through the burden of this encounter.

V. He gave His life for all.
R. He gave His life for me

This is the day when we picture the scene at Calvary, when we feel for Jesus the pain of the cruel nails, the agony of taut flesh, the life-blood draining away.

V. He gave His life for all.
R. He gave His life for me

This is the day when we hear again that triumphant cry, "It is finished!" -no longer a cry of dereliction but of victory over evil.

V. He gave His life for all.
R. He gave His life for me

God of the Cross, we pray:

May the eyes of our understanding be opened, that we may recognise the Gift of Life set before us.

May our hearts be ready to receive the Love You offer to us.

May our ears be unstopped that we may hear Your voice calling to us. And may our tongues be always ready to proclaim the Good News of the Gospel to all whom we meet.   Amen

33. A Good Friday Benediction

May the message of Jesus' passion and death on our behalf strengthen and sustain us till we meet again on the glorious day of resurrection. Amen

❖ ❖ ❖ ❖ ❖

34. A Personal Good Friday

Lord, when I think about the cross, not the bare wooden empty cross, too neat and polished to be of significance, but the rough cross on which You hung in agony, face distorted, blood running, body wracked with the pain of its own weight caught on two great nails through torn flesh, then I know it was for me You suffered so, and I'm ashamed at the thought of the little I put myself out for You.

Help me to understand it all, Lord, the real meaning of what You did as it affects me - and as I affect Your message now.

Then the veil was torn in two and all the wealth of shame and hypocrisy revealed. Now - now all that will come to light is my own inadequacy, my failure to love and serve You well.

Let me not crucify afresh Your memory but tell the world You love each one - and me.

35. A Litany for Holy Saturday

READING: *John 19:41-42 (RSV)*

"Now in the place where He was crucified there was a garden, and in the garden a new tomb where no one had ever been laid. So because of the Jewish day of Preparation, as the tomb was close at hand, they laid Jesus there."

The world is calm now. The storm came on cue and then the sunshine followed rain, renewing and refreshing the heavy air. This earth is part of God's creation, in which He reveals His glory to us.

V. For the day of Resurrection
R. We wait in faith and wonder

We have followed the events of Holy Week, witnessed betrayal, brutality, cowardice, but also the courage and conviction of the One who surrendered to death on the cross.

V. For the day of Resurrection
R. We wait in faith and wonder

All life waits, the day-to-day commerce of our world suspended in our minds as we anticipate the dawn of new life.

V. For the day of Resurrection
R. We wait in faith and wonder

The world can be a bitter place, where war and peace, hatred and love, concord and discord struggle side by side. The new life possible in Jesus conquers all boundaries, all bitterness and adversity.

V. For the day of Resurrection
R. We wait in faith and wonder

We do not forget that so many are in need. For them hope may be ebbing away - hope of food, shelter, love and livelihood. Others are sick and long for healing. *** Some are lonely, sad and depressed, and long for peace.

V. For the day of Resurrection
R. We wait in faith and wonder

Easter-time is a time for families, for renewing contact, for holidaying together, for beginning new life in marriage, and we remember those who will be married today. *** And those who have brought new life into the world in recent days. ***

V. For the day of Resurrection
R. We wait in faith and wonder

Above all, we wait for spiritual renewal; some of us will renew the vows made at our baptism; others will commit ourselves anew to whatever mission of service God calls us to undertake for Him.

V. For the day of Resurrection
R. We wait in faith and wonder

Lord, in our waiting, make us faithful, patient and full of loving anticipation.

Amen.

*** Where time and circumstances allow, names of individuals may be inserted here.

❖ ❖ ❖ ❖ ❖

36. Renewing our Vows

'In the Name of the Father and of the Son and of the Holy Spirit...'

Here, now, in the hush of Easter eve, when the world sleeps and dreams of eggs and Easter rabbits...

We keep vigil, waiting, praying, promising to serve. We are here remembering the vows our parents made that we should love You, serve You well and leave the world behind for You.

Here, now, as the candle flame flickers, grows, and casts its shadows all about, and each of us partakes one tiny light as symbol of our baptismal vows, we pledge ourselves afresh to serve You, follow on, and love You more.

❖ ❖ ❖ ❖ ❖

PART III: EASTER TO ASCENSION

EASTER DAY

37. Easter Praise

An angel said, "He is not here. He is risen."

Risen Lord Jesus, so many Easters have come and gone since those angels announced Your rising from death and yet the wonder of it is fresh and new every year.

Lord, accept our praise, listen as we glorify Your Name, as the bells proclaim to the world,

"He lives, oh yes, He lives and He has risen from the grave."

Lord, we praise and thank You for all You underwent on our behalf, the suffering, past now but leaving scars as reminders to us of what might have been but for You.

May our spirit of rejoicing this day be taken up and sung throughout the world, bringing love and peace and Easter joy to all people.

Amen.

38. Our Confession

Father God, in the spirit of Good Friday we were purged of sin against this Holy day, yet we know that no time has passed between that did not find us failing You.

We realise that we cannot spread the message of resurrection unless we are right with You, and so we confess our sins and ask Your pardon, for the sake of Your Kingdom here on earth.

Amen.

39. Prayers of Intercession for the Easter Season

"Come, share our Easter joy..." *

Lord God, Father of all, we come in thanksgiving for all that You are to us, yet all too aware that there are many people in the world for whom Easter joy is an unknown concept.

We pray for them -

Those who are homeless and destitute, victims of war and famine and of the rest of the world's greed.

Those who are unemployed and struggling to maintain their dignity.

Those who are disabled or chronically sick and feel that the world is passing them by.

Those who are facing long-term illness and others newly bereaved.

Those who are lonely, without direction and depressed.

Those who are in prison or persecuted without just cause, victims of hatred and violence, or racial abuse, and those whose culture or society keeps them down and suffocates their full potential.

Lord, where the needs of humanity are so great, may Your Gospel of love be made known in the meeting of physical as well as spiritual needs, that Your Name may be glorified in them, and Your Easter joy shed abroad in people's hearts.

Amen.

* F. Pratt Green

40. Personal Questions in the Garden

Lord, if I'd been there that first Easter morning, with Mary in the garden, would I have known You, or, like Mary, would I have mistaken You for someone else?

Then again, did Mary fail to recognise You out of disbelief, lack of expectation, because of her tears, or because You had changed?

And how would I have felt when You spoke to me and assured me it was You, come back to me - for me, for everyone?

Would I have felt overwhelmed, inadequate, shy even?

Or would I have lost all my inhibitions, shouted for joy, rushed to hug You..?

Lord Jesus, what if You walked into my line of vision right now, held up Your scarred hand and said, "Come?" What would I do then?

Lord, I am ashamed to think of it.

Forgive me - and come soon.

❖ ❖ ❖ ❖ ❖

41. Prayer for Good Shepherd Sunday

As we join in fellowship together to give thanks and to pray, to rejoice in God's goodness and experience His Love, we are reminded that in His presence is fulness of joy, that He is the source of all true pleasures, all true worth and wealth.

As we look out onto the natural world He has made for us to live and work in, and appreciate afresh the wonder of the tiniest creature, the renewal of earth after winter, the new life come to birth before our eyes, we know that His work is good and perfect.

As we seek that renewal of love, that spiritual firing to our hearts and lives, we are made more and more conscious of the cost of our freedom in a fettered world, of the possibilities life offers us in the exercise of our own God-given gifts, and would seek a greater appreciation and treasuring of them.

And as we become aware of all these gifts and wonders, we become even more aware of our own failures and shortcomings, of the sin and selfishness in the world about us, and of our inability to love others in Christ's Name, to be shepherds in His service, and we know our need for forgiveness and the will to be renewed in love.

Lord, grant us thankful hearts, minds at peace, lives so full of You that they overflow to all with whom we have to do and speak of Love.

❖ ❖ ❖ ❖ ❖

42. A Closing Prayer

Lord, the Light of Your Love is shining:
May it shine on us now,
Illuminate our lives,
and enable us to go forward in Your Name,
as shepherds to the lost,
leading them home
to You.

❖ ❖ ❖ ❖ ❖

ASCENSION

43. Ascension Vision

We believe in God - the Father
    God of God,
    Light of Light,
    True and Only God,
    Lord of heaven and earth,
    Creator and sustainer
    Of the whole universe.
God of all, we praise You.

We believe in God - the Son:
    King of Kings,
    Lord of Lords,
    Ascended in majesty,
    One with the Father,
    Judge of all,
    Friend of all,
    Drawing all people to Him.
Lord, our Lord, we praise You.

We believe in God - the Spirit:
    Spirit of Life,
    Power of Love,
    In us, around us,
    God in His world,
    Firing our vision,
    Sustaining our dreams,
    Making the impossible become reality.
Spirit of God, we praise You.

Father, Son and Holy Spirit,
    Giving us a place in creation,
    Vision and purpose in living,
    And a promise of glory to come.

Praise and glory and wisdom, thanksgiving and honour, power and might be to our God, for ever and ever.   Amen.

44. Petition for Ascensiontide

Risen and Ascended Lord,
Help us dream our dreams
As You fulfil Your vision in our lives,
And enable us so to live
that others may catch that vision through us.

Amen.

❖ ❖ ❖ ❖ ❖

45. Ascension Light
A Personal Prayer

Ascended Lord, grant me one moment of Your grandeur;
one precious glimpse of glory that will fire my heart
and make me speechless with wonder,
and afterwards to whisper,
"I love You."

❖ ❖ ❖ ❖ ❖

PART IV: PENTECOST AND TRINITY

PENTECOST

46. Praise and Confession

Lord, we come to You, singing Your praises,
Glorying in Your creation,
Remembering Your mercies,
Rejoicing in Your goodness to us.

What we have to offer in thanks is so paltry by comparison, and yet it
is what You would ask of us -

Our obedience,
respect,
faith,
dedication.

And what You give us is so wonderful, yet inexplicable,
incomprehensible, a Divine mystery wrought by Love -
Your Love, our Father God,
Your sacrificial saving Grace, Lord Christ,
Your indwelling presence, saving to the uttermost, now and
always, Holy Spirit, Light and Truth.

Lord, in the knowledge of all this, of what You are to creation and to
us, we are sorry that
our witness is so flawed,
our love so weak,
our commitment not wholly Yours.

We stand in awe,
we bow in gratitude;
we live in the assurance that when we are hurt by our own
failures, You forgive us
and enable us to go on living
in Your Love and care.

Amen

47. A Prayer of Confession

Lord God,
Like the Israelites of old we have set out to follow You,
but we have lost our way in the desert places of life.

Like Peter, we have sworn we would never forsake You,
but have lost sight of You in the crowds,
or disowned You in our embarrassment.

Like Paul, we have needed some blinding light to stop us in our tracks
and make us aware of Your presence.

> Father God, forgive us,
> redirect our paths,
> re-establish us in Your presence,
> renew our vision of hope in the future,
> through Your resurrection Love.   Amen

❖ ❖ ❖ ❖ ❖

48. Offering

> Living Bread,
> We hold out our hands,
> We offer you our hearts.
> May we not go home hungry
> but, filled with Your Spirit,
> Satisfied.

❖ ❖ ❖ ❖ ❖

49. Birthday Dedication

In dedicating our lives afresh,
May we be fit buildings for our Lord to inhabit,
Well-maintained, that we may commend Him by what we are,
And built on the firm foundation of His Love.

50. Responsive Praise

V. We are Your Church
R. And we praise You.

We come into Your presence, God, Holy One, conscious of Your Greatness, Your power, Your Glory, and of our own weakness, inadequacy and sin.

We come in awe. We come in wonder. We come aware of our unworthiness to be called Your people.

We thank You that even as we are aware of our need, You meet us where we are and offer Your forgiveness. We thank You for it, and all that You mean in our lives.

V. We are Your Church
R. And we praise You.

We come as the individuals who make up Your church here, in this (city/town/village), this community. Conscious of our imperfect example, we nevertheless offer ourselves to You in this worship, praying that You will use us together in the glorifying of Your Name.

V. We are Your Church
R. And we praise You.

We thank You for Your many gifts to us - as individuals and as a church - and especially the gift of New Life in Christ, freely available to all who seek. Help us, by our lives and witness, to make this gift known to those who are in need.

V. We are Your Church
R. And we praise You.

We offer You our life and work here, that all may be done in Your Name to Your glory; Your Word declared, Your Love proclaimed, lives changed because we are here, in faith, today.

V. We are Your Church
R. And we praise You.

51. Prayers of Intercession for the Renewal of the Church

Revelation Chs. 2 and 3

V.   Lord, send the Light of Your Love
R.   That the way ahead may be made clear.

Let us pray for the renewal of the Church.

As we are challenged by Your Word to the Churches in the first century, we pray that these may be a mirror to the Church of Christ today.

May it, as in every age, be Spirit led, seeking Your direction when the way seems dark and hopeless.

V.   Lord, send the Light of Your Love
R.   That the way ahead may be made clear.

Beset by gloom and despondency in the light of declining and ageing membership, we pray that we may yet look for positive signs under which to go forward.

May the people who make up the Church be ready and willing to follow Christ's leading, even to places they do not wish to go.

V.   Lord, send the Light of Your Love
R.   That the way ahead may be made clear.

As we continually read reports of factions and party lines, of confusions of dogmas and doctrines, we pray that Your word may still be heard above the squalls of dissent.

May the Spirit of peace and understanding, of truth and wholeness be permitted a place in Your House.

V.   Lord, send the Light of Your Love
R.   That the way ahead may be made clear.

As we turn from Your Word with the faults of the early churches still ringing in our ears, we pray that the lessons to be learnt from their mistakes may be real and lasting for our Church.

May we never, like Ephesus, lose our first love;

May we never, like Smyrna, judge our church life by the world's standards.

Unlike Pergamon, may we stand firm against devious and unorthodox practices.

Unlike Thyatira, may we refuse to give room to false prophets;

May we not, like Sardis, be inwardly dead;

Nor lukewarm, like Laodicea.

> V. Lord, send the Light of Your Love
> **R. That the way ahead may be made clear.**

Let us, instead, judge our church life in the light of the church that was praised for its loyalty and endurance.

May the Church of God everywhere be like Philadelphia, with an open door of welcome and a spirit of loving service and devotion.

> V. Lord, send the Light of Your Love
> **R. That the way ahead may be made clear.**

As we worship here today, the Church of Christ in this part of......, let us remember those of our members who need our special prayers...

> Our ministers...

> Those who are ill or depressed...
> whose relationships are fragmenting...
> who are lonely or grieving...
> and those with whom we can rejoice...

> Those who feel in need of forgiveness,
> or who cannot forgive;

> Those whose task is to care and heal,
> to be leaders and shepherds,
> organisers and administrators.

May the Spirit of Christ heal and bless and empower all those in need.

V.   Lord, send the Light of Your Love
R.   That the way ahead may be made clear.

Let us think, too, of the wider Church presence in the world, at home and overseas.

Those who head the various denominations, comprise the governing bodies and make often far-reaching decisions;

All those who fashion church policy and liturgy, and who are influential in shaping the image of Christ that the world in general has before it.

May they be on fire with zeal for Your cause and blessed with Your wisdom and power.

V.   Lord, send the Light of Your Love
R.   That the way ahead may be made clear.

And let us not, in our own preoccupations, forget those places where the Church is growing or facing hardship we could never envisage.

May we rejoice with those whose walls are bursting with enthusiasm,
Weep with those who are hurting;
Stand firm alongside those who are persecuted for speaking Christ's Name;
And pray with those who are facing opposition with courage and faith.

May the fire of God's Spirit fall on each one afresh, beginning with us, here, now.

Amen

52. Personal Pentecost

Holy Spirit of Power, breath of God, fire of Love,
enter my life today. Renew me, refresh me, redeem me,
empower me for Your service, to fulfil Your mission in
my own world for the extension of Your Kingdom.

Amen

TRINITY

53. Corporate Praise and Invocation

GOD, OUR FATHER, we come to You in the midst of the busy city, burdened with so many of the cares of the world:
>the sins of society,
>inhumanity and greed,
>hatred and selfishness,
>irresponsibility and lack of love.

Father, in the stillness, help us to give these burdens to You, that we may be free to praise You.

LORD JESUS CHRIST, we look to You from the uncertain road on which we travel, preoccupied with so many problems in the lives of those we love or seek to love:
>the sins of our neighbours,
>against us and each other,
>careless and indifferent,
>thoughtless and unloving.

Son of God, in the cold of the day, help us to unload our burdens and leave them at the foot of Your cross, that we may be free to love You.

HOLY SPIRIT, we seek Your power in the face of the helplessness we feel, our inadequacy to meet the needs of those who look to us:
>our sins of omission,
>self-centredness and fear,
>pride and arrogance,
>our offences and our defensiveness.

Spirit of Power, wind of God, glow into our hearts that we may be cleansed and absolved, that we may be empowered to serve You.

BLESSED AND HOLY TRINITY, Father, Son and Holy Spirit, we commit ourselves wholly to You, blessed to be a blessing in Your Name,
>cleansed of our sin,
>healed and whole,
>loving and loved,
>channels of Your peace.

Triune God, all powerful and good, be with us now, in all we say and do, that we may serve You through our service to Your world.

Amen

54. *Petitionary Prayer*

Lord God, You Who look down from the furthest reaches of the heavens:
> we reach up to You at this moment,
> in love and trust,
> knowing that You will hear.

Lord Jesus Christ, You who conquered death:
> Help us to conquer life,
> that with You we may be
> strengthened and enabled
> to reach our goal.

Holy Spirit, flowing from the Father through the Son and into our lives,
> You give us power when we are weak,
> Wisdom when we are in doubt:
> Illuminate our lives,
> Fill us with Your Love,
> One with us in our unity,
> Healing diversity.

May we together seek Your will today,
At peace one with another and with You,
Undefeated against the forces that seem greater than our understanding,
confident through the Hope You give us in Christ.   Amen

55. Trinity Praise
(based on Psalm 67)

Let the people praise You, O God,
Let all the people praise You...
For all You are,
For all You have done in creation,
For all You do for us, Your people,
day by day.

Let the people praise You, O God,
Let all the people praise You...
For all Your gifts:
Gifts of nature, time, relationships,
For the gifts given to each one to enable us to serve You
day by day.

Let the people praise You, O God,
Let all the people praise You...
For all things past,
For the present with its changes and chances,
For the future with its challenging uncertainty,
For each and every day.

Father, Son and Holy Spirit, Three in One, One in Three,
We praise You for Your Love,
We praise You for Your Life,
We praise You for Your Power,
Now and every day.

Amen

56. Praise to the One in Three

God, Father of all, we come to Your house,
into Your presence,
praising You for all that You are,
for the wonder of the world we live in,
in the hope of glory to come.

God, Son of God, Brother, Friend,
we draw close to You, one with You,
in thankfulness for the gift of life
made possible in Your great sacrifice of love,
for all, for ever, and for us.

God, Spirit of God, we pray Your power into our lives,
and through us into the world,
worshipping You for the precious gift,
in all its fulness, all joy and blessing,
all the love that comes from You alone.

God, Holy God, One in Three,
Father, Son, Spirit, all in all, all to all,
accept our offering of worship,
fill us with Your Love,
that others might meet with us
and catch a glimpse of Your glory in our lives.

Amen

57. *From the Beginning*

In the beginning - God...
    God, First, Last, in all, through all,
    We praise You for all You have made, all You are and have and do:
    Sight, sound, colour, song -
    songs of nature, songs of air and sea and land,
    One great chorus of Divinity.

"God so loved the world that He gave His only Son..."
    Jesus, high above all, King of kings, Lord of lords,
    present in creation, when all things were good,
    We praise You, we love You, we honour you
    for all You are to us, in our lives,
    for all You give to us day by day:
    Strength, hope, peace, joy,
    abundant life and Love,
    One great offering of Yourself.

"God... God is Spirit... God, the Spirit of God... come."
    We praise You, we reach out to You, call You, desire You;
    Come into our hearts and lives,
    fill us with Your Love, Your very being:
    Power, peace, beauty, Life:
    All that You have and are in us.

Father, Son, Holy Spirit, united with each trusting heart,
Come, take the praise of our hearts and lives and make them Yours,
               Make us Yours - always.

                                            Amen

PART V: OTHER TIMES AND SEASONS

ST. LUKE'S DAY (18th October) - LITURGIES FOR HEALING

58. Healing and Reconciliation

"But for you who fear My Name the sun of righteousness shall rise, with healing in its wings." *(Malachi 4:2)*

God promises His healing power to those who love and trust Him.

We come now to acknowledge that promise and to claim that power of healing in our lives, in our church, in our world.

V. Lord, through Your power
R. Heal us today.

"All this is from God, who through Christ reconciled us to Himself and gave us the ministry of reconciliation." *(2 Corinthians 5:18)*

Healing involves so many areas of our lives, not least our relationships with one another, in our homes, in the community and especially in the fellowship of the church.

Where we have fallen short in our relationship, we come now seeking reconciliation through the Love of Jesus by Whom all may be reconciled and be as one.

V. Lord, in Your Love
R. May we be one.

"(Jesus') fame spread... and they brought Him all the sick, those afflicted with various diseases and pain, demoniacs, epileptics, and paralytics, and He healed them." *(Matthew 4:24)*

Bodily healing is always uppermost in our minds, for that is healing which enables us to be fully functioning in our daily lives. God uses many means to our healing, from the skill of the surgeon to the touch of a hand in prayer.

We come now seeking that healing through the ministry of hands and hearts.

V. Lord, in Your power
R. Heal us, we pray.

"Jesus... went about doing good and healing all that were oppressed by the devil, for God was with Him." *(Acts 10:38)*

Mental and emotional sickness are harder to contain than the physical. Life becomes one dark tunnel of oppression and depression and the forces of evil weigh heavily upon us. But God is with us there in that tunnel, and His power overcomes the forces that would destroy us.

We come now to claim release from depression and the constant oppression on mind and emotions.

V. Lord, in Your Goodness
R. Deliver us, we pray.

"Beloved, I pray that all may go well with you and that you may be in health; I know that it is well with your soul." *(3 John v2)*

The greatest and most important area of healing for the Christian is that of the spirit. If we are right with God we know that He will never leave us without the strength to overcome all the threats to our health that the world may inflict upon us.

We come now, seeking God's will for our lives, committing ourselves to Him, regardless of cost, confident in His saving Grace and loving care for our souls.

V. Lord, in Your Grace
R. Use us, we pray.

"When he had spoken to me... I turned my face toward the ground and was dumb. And behold, one in the likeness of the sons of men touched my lips; then I opened my mouth and spoke. I said to him who stood before me, 'O my lord, by reason of the vision pains have come upon me, and I retain no strength. How can my lord's servant talk with my lord? For now no strength remains in me, and no breath is left in me.'

"Again one having the appearance of a man touched me and strengthened me. And he said, 'O man greatly beloved, fear not, peace be with you; be strong and of good courage.' And when he spoke to me, I was strengthened and said, 'Let my lord speak, for you have strengthened me.'" *(Daniel 10:15-19)*

With healing shall come peace - peace in our hearts, peace in our minds, peace in our bodies, and at peace within ourselves, we are at peace with our surroundings, with our colleagues in work and worship. He makes us strong enough to overcome.

As we draw our thoughts together, we look for peace in our lives, in our church, in our troubled world.

> V. Lord, in Your Mercy
> **R. Grant us Your peace.**

And so, with the prophet Jeremiah*, we affirm:

> **"Heal me, O Lord, and I shall be healed,
> save me, and I shall be saved."**

We pray not only for ourselves, but for others in need of healing:
for ***

*Jeremiah 17:14

*** Congregation to be invited to add their own requests here.

59. Prayers of Confession and Intercession on the Theme of Healing

Jesus looked at the cripple who had lain by the Pool of Bethesda for 38 years and said,   *"Take up your bed and walk...*
give up your sinful ways."

Lord God, as we put ourselves in the shadow of Your Light, we acknowledge the darkness of sin, the root of all spiritual sickness.

> **You, Lord, are a God of forgiveness:**
> **forgive us now, we pray,**
> **and make us whole in spirit.**

Faced with the man born blind Jesus touched his eyes. First he saw dimly, then with clear vision. Jesus sent this report of His activities to John: *"The blind recover their sight...*
the poor are brought good news."

Lord God, as we face the light of Your truth, we see, first dimly, and then fully the radiance of Your Truth.

> **You, Lord, are a God of Light,**
> **heal the blindness of our spiritual eyes,**
> **that we may see Your glory.**

The father brought his son to Jesus. "He has a spirit of dumbness. It throws him about and he gets hurt." Jesus spoke to it:

> *"Deaf and dumb spirit,*
> *I command you, come out of him and never go back."*

Lord God, we are like sheep before their shearers when we face You, dumb creatures, hardly able to verbalise Your praises.

> **You, Lord, are the God of all Truth.**
> **Loosen and then govern our tongues,**
> **that we may be enabled to proclaim that Truth.**

"How many of you are there?" asked Jesus of the spirits inhabiting the Gerasene demoniac. "A legion," they replied.
Jesus commanded,

> *"Out, unclean spirit,*
> *Come out of the man."*

48

Lord God, so often our minds are sick and we are unaware of it, for evil brings a subtle sickness.

You, Lord, are the God of Power.
By that power, free our minds
from all that makes us spiritually unhealthy

The man who was crippled from birth was let down through the roof by his friends. When Jesus saw their faith He said to the man,

"My son, Your sins are forgiven."

Lord God, we may be crippled in so many ways - in mind, body, emotions - and in turn our outlook on life and our relationships are also crippled.

You, Lord, have the power
to straighten what is bent,
to mend what is broken.
Make us whole.

The father's faith was challenged. It fell short. "I believe," he said, "Help my unbelief." Jesus would eventually say,

"Blessed are you who have not seen,
and yet have believed."

Lord God, we mar the completeness of our relationship with You by allowing doubt to brood and fester. We become imprisoned by our despair and disappointments.

You, Lord, have the power to release us from these bonds
and make us free.
Make us see our doubts dispelled
and faith made whole today.

The centurion came to Jesus and asked that his servant might be healed by the mere speaking of a word. Jesus was astonished.
"Truly I tell you, nowhere in Israel
have I seen such faith."

Lord God, Your Word is sufficient for our need. Help us to understand that. But we are here, while others may only hope at a distance.

**You, Lord, have the power of healing in a single word.
You are here, as You promised.
We bring to You now the names of those who cannot be here.
We may know some of their need. You know their real needs.**

(LEADER READS NAMES, followed by others spoken by members of the congregation.)

We pray that You will pour Your healing grace upon them. May they be renewed, refreshed, strengthened for their journey through life.

> **May they know that You are with them,
> know their doubts dispelled,
> their faith made whole.**

And as we who are here now come and claim Your blessing in our lives and the lives of those closest to us, may we experience the wonder of Your Love and care and the deep assurance of Your peace in our lives.   Amen

60. Prayers for Renewal and Healing

Note: *** denotes a period of silence, following which members of the congregation are invited to voice their particular concerns. Congregational responses are printed in bold.

"In Your steadfast love You led the people whom You redeemed; You guided them by Your strength..." *(Exodus 15:13)*

As we approach God in prayer we are made more aware of the greatness of His love for us and how He has led us, as He led Israel, in days past.

V.   Lord, make us more aware of Your presence in our lives;
R.   And strengthen us anew for Your service.

Even following news of the resurrection, the disciples hid behind closed doors, but Jesus came to them: "Peace be with you. As the Father has sent Me, so I send You." *(John 20:21)*

Let us pray for the peace of the world, for Christ's peace in the world, that there may be an end to all conflict as humanity learns to love and respect its neighbours.

V.   Lord, make us instruments of Your peace;
R.   And enable us to fulfil Your commission and service.

God, Alpha and Omega, beginning and end of all, has given us His promise: *"See, I am making all things new..."* *(Revelation 21:5)*

As we celebrate the new life offered in the Resurrection, symbolised by the renewal of nature, we are aware of our own need to be 'made new' by Him.

V.   Lord, open our eyes to the newness around us;
R.   And renew us by the power of Your Spirit.

Peter wrote, *"Blessed be the God and Father of our Lord Jesus Christ! By His great mercy He has given us a new birth into a living hope through the resurrection of Jesus Christ from the dead."* *(1 Peter 1:3)*

We come to Him, not as individuals only, but as the Church of God, His witnesses on earth. We pray that our individual and church life may be such that the new birth Christ has brought to us may be seen and sought after.

We pray for our ministers, our preachers, those who teach and those who learn, that together we may reflect Christ's resurrection promise to all with whom we have to do. ***

V.   Lord, encourage Your church, beginning here;
R.   And enable Your renewing power to be seen in us.

Paul, writing to the Galatians, declared, *"a new creation is everything."*
(Galatians 6:15b)

We acknowledge the needs of the world, of our country, of our own community. We see desperate need for healing, for reconciliation and renewal.

We pray for healing:

For those who are sick for the moment ***

For those who are chronically or terminally ill ***

For those recovering from operations, living on a knife edge, often, it seems, on borrowed time ***

For those whose wounds are mental or emotional, who are victims of abuse, or bereaved or lonely ***

For the misfits of society, those who will not or cannot seem to get it right ***

For those who are homeless and unemployed, whose despair has led to hopeless addiction ***

V.   Lord, remake and renew all whose lives are broken;
R.   through the redeeming power of Your Love.

So God, Father, Son and Holy Spirit, we seek Your Word and will for our lives, Your enabling and renewing power, as we bring our prayers and petitions to You, confident that You will hear and answer, in Your time and in Your way.

Help us, as we draw closer to You, to be ready and willing to be part of that answer.   Amen

61. A Liturgy of Healing for People and Places

Jesus said of His disciples, *"I pray for them... because they belong to You... While I was with them, I protected them by the power of Your Name, which You gave Me, and kept them safe ... It is not for these alone that I pray, but for those also who through the words put their faith in Me. May they all be one..."* (John 17:9, 12a, 20)

GOD WILLS THAT OUR RELATIONSHIPS SHOULD BE MADE WHOLE.

V.   Lord, receive our prayers,
R.   **And lead us to healing.**

WE PRAY for the churches in this community:
that they may be drawn closer together and work with one mind - that of Jesus Christ our Lord; that any factions within congregations might be united and bitter sores of conflict healed; that all Christians in the community may draw together and seek wholeness and reconciliation in order to enhance their mission and ministry to everyone.

V.   Lord, receive our prayers,
R.   **And lead us to healing.**

WE PRAY, too, for the people whose task is to maintain a spirit of wholeness within the churches, for ministers and lay leaders:
that the well-being of the whole of God's people in congregations may be paramount at all times; that personal preferences may be put aside; that personality problems might not dominate and create and sustain open wounds which fester and become dangerous sores.

V.   Lord, receive our prayers.
R.   **And lead us to healing.**

WE PRAY for the whole church family:
for the integration of groups with varying interests and priorities;
for young people, that they might experience a sense of belonging;
for families within the church, that they might find their fellowship in the Body of Christ a unitive force, and not a divisive one.

for the healing of broken relationships within both the church family and the individual families within it; for a greater sense of love and unity.

V.　Lord receive our prayers.
R.　And lead us to healing.

Jesus told His disciples, *"The time is coming when you will hear of wars and rumours of wars. See that you are not alarmed. Such things are bound to happen... For nation will go to war against nation, kingdom against kingdom; there will be famines and earthquakes in many places."*
(Matthew 24:6a, 7)
But the prophet Micah could also look to a time when, *"Nation will not take up sword against nation,"* but speak only peace.　*(Micah 4:3b)*

WE PRAY for the healing and reconciliation of broken relationships in the wider world:
> for warring factions in ...
> for corrupt regimes in ...
> in countries where troops are meting out senseless violence in the name of greed;
> for those continuing to practise sectarian violence...
> for those endeavouring to maintain peaceful relationships where there is continual unrest...

V.　Lord, receive our prayers.
R.　And lead us to healing.

WE PRAY for those caught up in violence and warfare, those made homeless, others hungry and struggling to survive:
> for the refugees in ...
> for people suffering homelessness and deprivation...
> for girls and women abused in war...
> for those who are victims of circumstances rather than choice, who long for the privilege once more to live as families in their own homes;
> for all victims of abuse, especially young people subjected to incest and violence at home, and those exposed to the degrading and damaging rituals of Satanism - particularly those suffering today who yesterday were whole people.

for minority groups who have genuine causes to fight yet no voice with which to make their claims heard.

V.   Lord, receive our prayers.

R.   **And lead us to healing.**

On the eve of the Passover Jesus told His disciples, *"You will all lose faith; for it is written, 'I will strike the shepherd and the sheep will be scattered'..."*   *(Mark 14:27)*

WE COME IN PRAYER especially for those churches without a shepherd, in many cases lost and fragmenting. We pray:

for healing of the divisions in congregations;

for a greater sense of mutual understanding within congregations, especially in smaller churches where this causes such strife;

for churches dominated by the rival claims of long-standing family feuds;

for churches from which active leaders have been moved, or have become engulfed in conflicting activities;

for churches where young and old vie for supremacy, creating more wounds and tension;

for the churches leaning on one family for leadership, and for the families involved, that they may not be placed under greater stress.

V.   Lord, receive our prayers.

R.   **And lead us to healing.**

And WE PRAY for our own shepherd...

may she/he receive Your help and strength at all times

Your guidance when difficult decisions have to be made

the love and support of family and friends;

the continual knowledge that she/he is loved and supported by those to whom she/he has ministered;

the wisdom and compassion to be a bearer of Your healing power to all in need.

V.   Lord, receive our prayers.

R.   **And lead us to healing.**

WE PRAY now for others we know of in any need, by whom or for whom prayer has been asked today:

ONE WORLD WEEK

62. Praise for God's World

God, Creator, Sustainer and Friend of all people,
We bring our prayers and bless Your Name.

God, Holy, Mighty and One Who cares,
Human words are inadequate to describe You,
Our thoughts too narrow
to measure the depth
and height and breadth
of Your great Love for us.

God of Peace and Justice,
in Whom all are one,
through Whom all may move toward reconciliation,
equal in Your sight,

May we, in our worship of You,
look beyond ourselves
to Your created world,
and see, not squalor and ugliness,
but a vision of the beauty
You intended us to see,
and challenge us, this day,
to work toward bringing that vision
to reality.   Amen

63. Prayer of Confession

Father God, we come with a new awareness
of our place in the world,
our responsibility for justice,
for caring for those in need.

Forgive us the times we have failed them.

Father God, we come, conscious of our inactivity
our unwillingness to move forward
in love and trust,
and to go out of our way
to show Your love to the unloved.

Forgive us the times we have failed You.

Father God, we come, knowing our own weakness,
too self-conscious to be aware of others,
blind to their hurting through our own hurts,

Forgive us that we have not put our need into Yours hands.

Father God, unite us now in the hope of the world,
and in the knowledge that You are a forgiving God,
on Whom all may depend.

Amen

REMEMBRANCE DAY

64. In Praise of God Who Remembers

Let us praise God together.

"Great God of wonders - ALL Your ways display Your attributes divine."

We praise You for Your Goodness;
We praise You for Your Grace;
We praise You that we, in all our insignificance, are able to approach You, talk with You, and hear You speaking to us today,
and that what we know of You enables us, when we seek Your help, to work together with You.

You are a worker of miracles:
grant us the faith to believe,
the vision to see,
and the boldness to ask for the miraculous in our lives.

You are an active God, Who works with us and answers our prayers; help us to be attuned to You, that together we may tell the world of your wonders.

You are a God Who remembers us when we feel lost and forsaken,
Who comes to us in our times of need,
Who companions with us on the journey through life.
Help us to remember today all Your goodness to us, even in those times when we thought You had left us, but instead were working quietly among us.

May we focus our thoughts on the past only when it gives us cause to praise You,
the present because we know You are still with us in all our concerns,
and the future because we know that whatever happens You will still be there, the same yesterday, today and forever.

And so we commit this act of worship to You, praising You,
and remembering above all things the Victory of our Lord Jesus Christ over death, through His Cross and resurrection.

Amen

65. In Perspective

"At the going down of the sun, and in the morning, we will remember..."

Lord God, this is the day when we remember so many past events, people we have known and loved who are gone from us, some taken out of season as a result of humankind's inhumanity.

We come today, not to praise great and famous men, but to praise You, Lord, for giving us this day, for our freedom, and even in a world continuing in war and unrest, for the peace which we do have, as a nation and as individuals.

Let us commemorate this day, not as a relic of the past, but as a sign of hope for the future, for while we remember human sacrifice, we remember, too, the divine sacrifice of Jesus on the cross which makes our peace and freedom possible.

It is for that above all that we praise You today.

66. Act of Confession for Remembrance Day

Let us come to God in penitence:

God declared to Moses,
"I AM the Lord... I am mindful of My Covenant."

FATHER GOD, we come to You today, mindful of our own weakness before You, our reluctance to believe in Your promises, to accept that You answer prayer, even when the answer is not what we hope for.

V.   Forgive us, we pray
R.   **Help us to remember the Victory.**

LORD JESUS CHRIST, You gave Your life that we might live free of the threat of eternal death, but we forget so easily, and fail to remember the enormity of that sacrifice, and of Your love for us.

V.   Forgive us, we pray
R.   **Help us to remember the Victory.**

HOLY SPIRIT of God, bringer of hope, of peace, of love, on this day when we remember human enmity and inhumanity in their most violent and extreme proportions, we are conscious of our inability to forgive those who have wronged us, by action or inaction, through words spoken or deeds done; of our broken relationships, our insensitivity and lack of care for others, our own disbelief and hopelessness.

V.   Forgive us, we pray
R.   **Help us to remember the Victory.**

Father, Son and Holy Spirit, as Your Church, Your visible presence in the community, we are conscious of our failure to reach out to those around us in hope, in peace and in love; our lack of positive witness, in our failure to bring the Good News of freedom to those in bondage to the world, to tell them that we love them in Your Name.

V.   Forgive us, we pray
R.   **Help us to remember the Victory.**

Affirmation
We have the promise that all who ask in penitence and faith shall receive. We claim the victory through Christ our Lord.

Thanks be to God. Amen

67. *Prayers of Intercession for Remembrance Day*

We come before God, remembering the past,
but conscious of the needs of the present.
Rejoicing in our freedom,
we remember those in bondage,
the hostages of the world,
those in fear,
those caught in the traps of poverty and debt,
through unemployment, homelessness,
through inability to cope with the pressures of life....

Rejoicing in our comparative peace,
we remember those who live in areas of war and unrest,
those involved in peace initiatives,
those attempting to police the trouble spots of the world...

Rejoicing in our homes and families,
we remember those whose homes are torn apart by grief and dissension,
inability to relate, disturbances, selfishness, sown with the seeds of self-destruction.

Rejoicing in our freedom to worship and witness,
we remember those whose lips must remain sealed,
whose church doors are barred,
who daily face death in their Christian walk.

Rejoicing in our place in the Body of Christ on earth,
We remember our church and its ministers and those who even now are being called and confirmed in ministry, especially those whom we know, who are close to us;
let us remember always to uphold them in our prayers and in our actions, when together we may work for the furtherance of Your glorious Kingdom here on earth.

Amen.

68. Responsive Prayers of Intercession for Remembrance Sunday

These prayers aim to focus on the many areas in which we are commanded to remember the precepts and promises of God in our Christian lives.

> V.   Lord, we remember in Love;
> R.   **Let us always be faithful.**

The Preacher of Wisdom urged his hearers to *"Remember Your Creator in the days of your youth, before the bad times come and the years draw near when you will say, 'I have no pleasure in them'..."* *(Ecclesiastes 12:1)*

But Moses urged also, *"Remember the days of old, think of the years, age upon age; ask your father to inform you, the elders to tell you. When the Most High gave each nation its heritage..."* *(Deuteronomy 32:7-8a)*

It is so easy to get caught up in the excitement of life and to forget Who gave us that life.

LET US REMEMBER TO THANK GOD....

- for the gift of life;
- for the excitements of childhood which those who are young enjoy daily, and those who are older may remember with pleasure;
- for the opportunities we experience - new ways of learning, seeing, doing and being;
- for new friends to be made, even as we mourn the loss of older ones, through moving away or through death;
- for the constant reminder of God's goodness to us as individuals, for the times when we say with feeling,
  'There but for the Grace of God go I....'
- for the opportunities to live out our faith in compassionate action towards others;
- for...***

> V.   Lord, we remember in Love;
> R.   **Let us always be faithful.**

The Lord instructed His people to *"Remember to keep the sabbath day holy. You have six days to labour and do all your work; but the seventh day is a sabbath to the Lord your God."* *(Exodus 20:8-10a)*

Seven whole days do make one weak - seven whole days of constant worldly activity, when we can become spiritually fatigued.

LET US REMEMBER:

o   that God is the God of all life:
o   that as Christians our whole lives must be committed to Him, our every activity, worldly or worshipful, must be dedicated to His glory;

o   that the church is not just for Sundays, but that it exists in the community to serve the needs of the other six days - the needs of those who are lonely, who have problems, who are younger, with time on their hands and little to fill it, and for those who want to give more than service;

o   that it is Christ's command that we meet together in His Name, to break bread, share in fellowship and worship, and mutual spiritual support, for this is vital to our corporate witness as His Church.

V.   Lord, we remember in Love;
R.   **Let us always be faithful.**

The Lord *"remembered us when our fortunes were low - His love endures for ever - and rescued us from our enemies; His love endures for ever. He gives food to all mankind; His love endures for ever."*   (Psalm 136:23-25)

We are constantly reminded of the needs of the wider world, where often Christ is not known, and the gods worshipped are those of greed and selfishness.

LET US REMEMBER:

o   to thank God for the freedom we have to live and work and worship as we choose;

o   that there are many in this world today who are still denied the right to worship as they would, to live out what they believe openly;

o   that there are countless people suffering through both man-made and natural disasters - through war, earthquakes, famine, exploitations, especially at this time in...***

o   that there are many people violating the human rights of others, imprisoning without charge, inflicting cruelty and persecution, punishment for no cause - people who need leading to the truth, who need understanding and forgiveness - especially today in ...***

o that there are those perpetuating racial and sectarian conflicts who need to be brought to an understanding of true unity and equality in Christ - especially today in...***

o that we who have so much freedom may never forget the price paid for it, and so may be willing to do all we can for those still in need as a result of that payment - for the long-term wounded; for war widows; for...***

V.   Lord, we remember in Love;
R.   **Let us always be faithful.**

"Remember your leaders..."   *(Hebrews 13:7)*

The writer to the Hebrews was thinking more in terms of church leaders, but we who live in the free world often forget our responsibility to those who govern us, especially when we disagree with their actions.

LET US, THEREFORE, REMEMBER:

o those in government over us - the Prime Minister, members of Parliament, local leaders of all authorities and government bodies.

o members of the Royal Family who are our ambassadors to other countries, and yet are human as we are and have their own problems and needs;

o those who have influence on world affairs, Euro-M.P.s, members of the United Nations, leaders of other major nations; all those in any way involved in the world's decision-making programmes - May all make informed decisions, right choices, and seek just solutions to all problems.

V.   Lord, we remember in Love;
R.   **Let us always be faithful.**

The Lord asked, *"Is Ephraim still so dear a son to Me, a child in whom I so delight that, as often as I speak against him, I must (remember) him again? Therefore My heart yearns for him; I am filled with tenderness for him."*

(Jeremiah 31:20)

As a worshipping, caring Christian community, we must always be mindful of the needs on our own doorstep, often less obvious than the crushing needs of the world, and yet areas in which we may exercise both practical and spiritual help.

WE REMEMBER:

o those in our community who are sick or suffering from long-term diseases or disability...***
o those who are anxious...***
o those who have difficult decisions to make...***
o those who feel hurt or rejected...***
o those who have been bereaved...***
o those who are suffering from the breakdown of family relationships...***

     V.   Lord, we remember in Love;
     R.   **Let us always be faithful.**

The dying criminal called out from his cross, *"Jesus, remember me when You come to Your throne."*   *(Luke 23:42)*

Our ministers and leaders, Jesus' representatives among us, on whom we rely for both leadership and intercession, are a vital source of inspiration for our work; therefore, we must never forget the mutual responsibility we have in supporting them.

WE REMEMBER NOW:

those who lead us in worship week by week, our ministers and lay preachers;
those who have pastoral responsibility, ministers and lay people;
those who have the spiritual care of this congregation...***
those who are chaplains at our local hospitals and institutions, industrial companies, and the prison:
those who have gone from this church into the wider ministry of the church, both home and overseas, especially ...***
those involved in secular ministry in the community, especially...***

     V.   Lord, we remember in Love;
     R.   **Let us always be faithful.**

"Remember, therefore, the teaching you received; observe it, and repent."
     (Revelation 3:3)

And we pray for ourselves, that we, too, may be remembered before God, and may work together with Him to the glory of His Kingdom.

V. Lord, we remember in Love;
R. **Let us always be faithful.** Amen

*** Current and local names and needs may be inserted at these points.

69. Personal Memories

Lord,

in remembering the past,
help me to dwell on the positive events and not the negative ones;

in remembering the people who have passed through my life,
help me to remember the good things about them and not the bad,
to think of them, not with hatred but with love;

in remembering the hurts I have suffered,
help me to remember the healing and not the wounds;

in looking back,
help me to go forward and not to sink in nostalgia,
to treasure visions for the future and not dreams of the past.

Amen

70. Prayers of Confession and Intercession for All Saints' Day

with sung response

The response is the Taize chant, as in Songs and Hymns of Fellowship, New Edition, No 243...

O Lord, hear my prayer...

The Lord hears our prayers and will have compassion on those who come to Him in faith,

O Lord, hear my prayer...

Our Father God, we come,
> not as saints but as sinners in need of Your forgiveness,
> forgiveness for our greed in the face of others' need,
> forgiveness for our arrogance in the face of Christ's humility,
> forgiveness for our inability to love and forgive our enemies and those who hurt us;
> and for our carelessness towards our friends and those who love us;
> forgiveness for the many times we have failed to proclaim
> Christ by our lives,
> and have been ashamed to confess His Name with our lips.
> For all these failures we seek Your word of peace.

The Lord hears our prayers and will have compassion on those who come to Him in faith.

O Lord, hear my prayer...

Lord Jesus, Christ of the World, Lord of our lives, as we stand in Your presence we are aware of Your forgiving, cleansing love, and we thank You for it. Help us, in the light of that love, to recognise the needs of our world,
> a world torn apart
> by greed and selfishness;
> lust for power,
> war and bloodshed,
> hatred and violence.
> Help us to be agents of light in the darkness of sin,
> bringers of peace into the restless places.

The Lord hears our prayers and will have compassion on those who come to Him in faith.

O Lord, hear my prayer...

Holy Spirit of God, witnessing with our Spirit to the truth that is in Christ, make us, Your Church on earth today, aware of the needs of others:
those who are hungry and homeless,
sick and dying,
hopeless and destitute,
lonely and unloved,
victims of war and famine,
of humankind's inhumanity to its own.
Help us to love them in the Name of Christ,
and through our lives make Him known to them.

The Lord hears our prayers and will have compassion on those who come to Him in faith.

O Lord, hear my prayer...

Father, Son and Holy Spirit, One God, powerful Creator, as we gaze on Your awesome presence, so direct our eyes towards Your creation, and help us to see fresh visions of hope where there is death and destruction,
pollution and neglect,
immorality and disease,
despair and hopelessness.
Grant us grace so to be like Christ our Lord and pattern, that we may be vessels of hope in the empty places, that they may be filled with Your presence.

The Lord hears our prayers and will have compassion on those who come to Him in faith.

O Lord, hear my prayer...

Triune God, Head of Your Church Triumphant, look upon Your Church on earth, help us to see our real needs, especially our need of You, and make us ministers of Your Grace to those in need at this time:

those who are sick and infirm,
disabled in mind, body or spirit,
those oppressed by fear and anxiety,
those who need loving arms and a shoulder to cry on,
those who are bereaved and alone.
Help us, that together we may witness to the sanctity of Your love,
continuing as one heart and life with those who have gone before us,
whom we celebrate in our hymns, seek to emulate in our lives and long
to be with throughout eternity.

The Lord hears our prayers and will have compassion on those who come
to Him in faith.

O Lord, hear my prayer...   **Amen**

MISSION

71. A Prayer of Approach

We come into the presence of the God Who calls, commissions and uses ordinary people to fulfil His great mission of Love on earth.

We acknowledge His power infilling and surrounding us, His authority over us, His unfailing care for us and for all people.

We praise Him for His saving work, for the love that reaches out to each one of us, breathes into us, and says, "I care for you. You matter to Me."
Great God of wonders, from the centre and perfection of Your creation we praise You for all You are to us, all You give to us, all Your care for us, now, and then and in times to come.

We commit this act of worship to You. Guide us, call us, draw us nearer to Your presence, and so work in us that those who meet us will know that we are walking with You, every step of the way.

Amen

72. Working Together with God
Prayers of Intercession on the Theme of Mission.

St Paul wrote to the Corinthians, *"Working together with Him, we entreat you not to accept the grace of God in vain."* (2 *Corinthians 6:1, R.S.V*)

Yet God's Grace is free and abundant to all who seek Him, and this is the message we are called upon to take out into the world.

V. Working together with God
R. Let us build His Kingdom on earth

Jesus told His disciples, *"Everyone will hate you for your allegiance to Me."*
(Matthew 10:22)

Discipleship is costly. It demands a level of life and commitment beyond the natural capabilities of mere humanity - but the Grace of God enables men and women to respond to that call, as they have done in every age.

V.   Working together with God
R.   **Let us be bold to respond to His call**

Jesus sent out His disciples on a mission, two by two (Luke 10:1) - different people with different outlooks on life, and different gifts to offer in His service.

Throughout history God has brought together in unity many diverse people and opinions, individuals and groups, with one common end in view.

V.   Working together with God
R.   **Let us establish unity one with another in His Name.**

Paul wrote that within the local church there are many ministries in addition to that of the apostolate - prophecy, teaching, healing, caring, administration, the charismatic gifts of working miracles and speaking in and interpreting tongues.   (1 Corinthians 12:4-10)

If we are to be effective witnesses to Him in the local community we cannot work in isolation, but together we can pool those gifts in one great offering to Him.

V.   Working together with God
R.   **Let us build His Kingdom here**

Jesus exhorted His disciples to *"Proclaim the Kingdom of God and to heal the sick."*   *(Luke 9:2)*

Mission in the local community is not divorced from the problems of everyday living. We are called as the church together in this place to go out to people and meet their needs wherever they are, and especially today we remember those we know who are in need...***

V.   Working together with God
R.   **Let us bring healing where it is needed,**
       friendship in loneliness,
       love where there is hatred,
       peace to the violent places.

Jesus calls some to be prophets, some preachers and teachers...
                                                    (1 Corinthians 12:28)

We need to hold in our prayers all those with special ministry in the church, locally and nationally, for...***

V.   Working together with God

R.   **Let us unite in the bonds of prayer,**
give support to all in need,
and build bridges of love over things
that divide us.

Paul wrote to the Church in Rome, "*Conform no longer to the pattern of this present world, but be transformed by the renewal of your minds.*"

(Romans 12:2)

The Church exists in the world, a world which rejects all it stands for - truth, goodness, love, peace. Let us not shirk our responsibility in prayer and action on behalf of all in authority, locally, nationally, internationally, that commonsense and sound judgment may prevail, and the good of everyone be considered at all times.

V.   Working together with God

R.   **May we help make the world a better place**

"*He has said, 'In the hour of My favour I answered you; on the day of deliverance I came to your aid.'*"   *(2 Corinthians 6:2)*

So we commit this place (town/city, etc.) to God, asking that opportunities will be revealed in which we may demonstrate His abundant Grace and our real unity of purpose in Christ, and play our part in fulfilling His great commission here on earth.

V.   Working together with God

R.   **We commit these prayers to You now, in the Name of our**
Lord and Saviour, Jesus Christ.
                            Amen.

***   There will be an opportunity for members of the congregation to include specific names and concerns.

73. A General Prayer

Lord, we pray for the world in which we live:
Where there is war, help us to bring peace.
Where there is discord, help us to bring unity.
Where people are homeless, help us to give them shelter.
If they are lonely and destitute, help us to befriend them.
Where they are imprisoned by evil forces, help us to penetrate the barriers
with Your Love and Power.
And whoever is sick, use us in their healing.
Whoever is lost, enable us to find.
Whatever a person's need let us not be blind or deaf to it.
Enable us to be at one with You, Lord, and with each other, that Your Spirit
may be experienced through us.

Amen.

PRAYERS ON THE THEME OF JUSTICE
74. A Litany of Praise

"My chains fell off, my heart was free"*

Let us praise God that we can come to worship in freedom;
Let us rejoice that our lips need not be sealed,
nor our voices silent,
Let us be thankful that we have hearts and emotions
generous and sensitive enough to recognise
Christ's suffering and our need,
And His need of our love.

> **R.** **We come now with thankfulness**
> **For all we have and are in Him,**
> **For His suffering Love**
> **That sets us free.**

Let us praise God that we are not bound by law,
but by His free Grace;
Let us rejoice that we may be
free of worldly shackles,
that we have no need for fear;
Let us be thankful that all the channels of communication
are wide open
for us to receive from Him
and in receiving give our all in return.

> **R.** **We come now with thankfulness**
> **For all we have and are in Him,**
> **For His suffering Love**
> **That sets us free.**

* Charles Wesley

75. A Prayer of Confession

Lord Jesus Christ,
> You take from us the wooden yoke of manipulation
> and the iron yoke of slavery to sin:
> Forgive us when we cling to these.

> You offer us eternal life, deliverance from evil,
> Protection from our own mortality:
> Forgive us when we do not understand.

> Your Word is Truth, Your promises to us are unconditional,
> Your Spirit sets us free, Your grace suffices us:
> Forgive us when we cannot believe.

> If we are in Christ we are His new creation,
> Free in Him, kept by His Love,
> Made one with Him, as heirs of His promises:
> Help us to know the truth and be free.

Amen

BIBLE SUNDAY

76. Prayers for Bible Sunday

"The Word of the Lord endures for ever."*

Let us praise God that we have freedom to open the Bible and share its message with others at any place or time.

Your Word is a lamp to my feet, a light on my path.

But we remember those to whom the Bible is a closed book, praying that God will enable it to be opened for them and that they may receive His message in their hearts.

Father, hear our prayer.

Let us praise God that the barriers to the free access of His Word have broken down in so many countries, especially in Eastern Europe.

How sweet is the taste of Your instructions - sweeter even than honey... Your commands more than gold, even the finest gold.

Yet there are still many areas in the world where it is difficult to obtain a Bible, and we remember now the work of the Bible Society, the Scripture Gift Mission, the Pocket Testament League and others who work tirelessly to carry God's Word to those who need it.

Father, hear our prayer.

Let us praise God that more people than ever before have the benefit of even a basic education and that for many it opens up the Word of God to them.

Your Word is revealed, and all is light; it gives understanding even to the untaught.

But we also remember that there are still nearly 3,000 tongues in which there is no Bible, and we think of those whose lives are committed to the work of translation, especially the Wycliffe Bible Translators.

Father, hear our prayer.

Let us praise God for all that His Word has meant to us in our lives, all that it may mean to others in times of need and uncertainty, and for the faithful preaching and propagation of His Word by all means possible.

Your instruction is my continual delight; I turn to it for counsel... I have put my hope in Your Word.

In this we remember the work of pastors and Bible Society workers who travel many miles by bicycle in remote African countries to enable people to have Bibles of their own; for the Gideons who seek to ensure that many more people have access to the Word of God in public places.

Father, hear our prayer.

Let us be thankful for all who give their time, talents and possessions to help further the ministry of the Word.

Open my eyes, so that I may see the wonderful truths in Your law.

We bring our reasons for praise and the needs for which we pray to You, our God and Father, believing that You will hear and answer according to Your gracious will, through Jesus Christ our Lord.

Your Word is founded in steadfastness, and all Your just decrees are everlasting.

* A line from Roger Jones: Greater than Gold.

77. A Bible Sunday Thanksgiving

Let us thank God today
> For His Word,
> uttered out of the void,
> creative force in the universe,
> written,
> spoken,
> revealed to us in and through His Son, Jesus Christ.

Let us thank God today
> For the manifestation of His Son,
> Who came to earth as a symbol of reconciliation,
> Whose saving act is made known
> in the written Word of the Bible
> for us and for posterity.

Let us thank God today
> For access to His Word
> in so many translations and forms,
> for our freedom to open the Book,
> to read,
> to share
> in any place, at any time.

Let us thank God today
> For those who carry this Word to others who
> have not heard,
> Messengers of Good News,
> translators of peace,
> forerunners and instruments
> of His continuing work.

Let us thank God today
> for the privilege of meeting together as His people
> one in His Name,
> in His Love,
> receivers of all He has to give.

Let us thank God today
for all the knowledge His Word brings to us,
for those dedicated to the task of interpreting the Word.
aiding our understanding,
inspiring and directing us.

We rejoice in this Word,
the Gift and the Giver -
and offer this act of worship as a token
of our response.   Amen

78. Prayer of Confession and Intercession on the Theme of Unity

"Jesus, united by Thy grace,
and each to each endeared,
With confidence we seek Thy face
*and know our prayer is heard."**

We come to this time of prayer, conscious that our efforts to unite with others are so weak by comparison with the great potential there is for working together in the world.

Father God, forgive us for lost opportunities through our own half-hearted approach to united witness.

We acknowledge that we talk much of unity as a future possibility yet inwardly we are clinging to our own past traditions.

Lord, forgive us, and help us to catch a vision of the future in the here and now, so that we may be enabled to shake off those things from the past that hinder our present witness.

We confess that we have neglected opportunities to work and witness together and often encouraged dissent by our unwillingness to see the other church's point of view or understand what they are saying.

Lord, You would have us united as one in proclaiming Your Word, not only by our words but by all we do together. Forgive us where we have failed.

Even within our own church we have permitted self - or group interest to cloud our unity of purpose and have allowed the world outside to witness our fragmentation instead of a demonstration of Christ's love through us.

Forgive us, Father, when we have allowed our own petty grievances and desires to over-ride what is best for the church as a whole.

There are times when we have failed in our witness and service to individuals in need because we have not recognised that we are one family and so have denied our responsibility and left them by the wayside.

Lord, forgive us when we have failed to give words of comfort, a hand to help, or a listening ear to those in need.

80

Father God, we praise You because You are a God who forgives sins even when Your people seem unable or unwilling to be so forgiving.

Thank You, for Your forgiveness. May we not neglect the forgiving of others in Your Name.

In acknowledging these failures, we pray now for those whom we know, in and out of church, who are in need in any way... ***

Lord, hear our prayer and grant Your healing power to their lives.

We pray for those who work and worship in other churches in this neighbourhood... ***

Help us, Lord, to seek ways in which we may work together rather than in competition with them, in the sharing of common interests and resources, to help rather than hinder the work of Your Kingdom in this area.

We pray for the wider church in the world, for its ministry in areas where there is great opposition to the Christian Gospel.

May all who confess Your Name be able to unite in love to combat the forces that would destroy the Church and wipe the Name of Jesus from all lips.

We pray for the Bible Society, The Scripture Union and other agencies that encourage people to read and explore Your Word, whose activities cut across our denominational boundaries and reach out to the whole community.

May all who work in this way experience the oneness of spirit that comes form being where You want them to be.

So may we who bring these prayers today become aware of our part in God's answer to them.

Father, help us to be aware of Your voice, guiding and empowering us in our lives and service, that we ourselves may not stand in the way of the unity we seek.

> "Touched by the lodestone of Thy love,
> Let all our hearts agree,
> And ever t'ward each other move,
> And ever move t'ward Thee."*

*   Charles Wesley: H & P No.773
***   **Members of the congregation are invited to contribute names and concerns known to them.**

PART VI: GENERAL PRAYERS

79. A Prayer of Approach

Let us come into the stillness of the Presence of God,
leaving aside all our earthly preoccupations,
our troubles and difficulties,
the things that cause us hurt and anxiety.

Let us seek the Peace of God in our hearts and lives,
the power of His Spirit to enable us,
the power of His Word to guide us;
His Love to comfort and encourage us.

Let us seek His will for us;
His purpose in our lives,
the desire and ability to go out to others and serve them
in the way He would have us serve.

May none of us feel alone and inadequate,
but know that with Him all shall be possible,
all SHALL be well.

❖ ❖ ❖ ❖ ❖

80. A 'Meeting' Prayer

Lord God, we come, on this (glorious) day to offer You our praises for what You are and for what You reveal of Yourself in Your created world.

To give You our thanks for what You give to us so freely - far more than we may ask or deserve.

To ask forgiveness for the many ways in which we have squandered Your gifts to us and marred Your created work.

To pray for those who do not recognise You in Your world, who have not encountered the wonder of redeeming grace, the Power of Your Spirit in their lives.

To offer ourselves - all that we have and are, to Your service, in whatever way You call us.

Amen

81. Praise to the Living God

Praise to the Living God,
Praise, honour, worship and blessing
be to You, our God, as we meet together today.

We see Your glory revealed in Your created world,
but our words are inadequate to describe it;

We see the many evidences of Your love in our world,
but our eyes are too dim to penetrate the reality.

We hear the music of Your world in natural things,
but our ears are too full of the world's discordant notes.

We feel the wonder of Your presence in our hearts,
but keep the knowledge a secret because we are too surprised to share it.

Living, Loving Father,
May our eyes and our ears,
our lips and our hearts
be open to You afresh today,
that we may declare the wonders of Your creation
through the miracle of Your Love in us.

Amen.

82. A Holiday Fellowship Prayer

Father God, we thank You that out of Your great goodness You make this time of fellowship possible;

that out of Your great love for us You gave us Your Son to be our Saviour, to lead us as a shepherd, walk with us on the way, and open up the path to eternal life.

Thank You that You have given us this new day in which to tell others Your message,

that through Your Spirit we may be enabled to reach out in Your Love.

Amen.

83. A Morning Prayer

Father, we come to You today,
praising You for Your great goodness,
conscious of Your glory, Your might, Your power,
and of our own weakness, inadequacy and sin.
And yet we know that You love us,
and in this knowledge we confess our faults,
and ask Your forgiveness,
confident that You will hear and heal and save us.

We thank You for bringing us together in worship and fellowship
at the beginning of another week,
and we pray that You will be with us when we go from here,
to our homes, our places of work and study and recreation.

> God,
> In whose image we are created:
> help us so to honour Your Name,
> that all may see in us Your likeness,
> and render to You the glory which is due:
> Through Jesus Christ our Lord.

Amen

84. Prayer before Worship

Our Father God,
we thank You that we are able to worship You here today.

> We praise You for Your goodness,
> We praise You for Your Love;
> We thank You for Your mercy and compassion,

for all the wonderful gifts of life you shower upon us.

May we be conscious of Your hand always on our lives,

> leading us,
> guiding us,
> healing us,
> blessing us,

that we may walk with You every step of the way.

Enrich our worship today, we pray.
Help us to glorify Your Name
     in this building,
     in this town
     by our lives.

Come to us, we pray, and touch us with Your Spirit,
that we and all we know may see that we have been with You,
and that we are so blessed
that we may become a blessing to others.

Amen

❖ ❖ ❖ ❖ ❖

85. Evening Praise

We Praise You, O God,
We acknowledge You to be the Lord:
God of Nature,
God of the Universe,
Lord of our lives.

We thank You, O God,
That You have given us this day,
A new beginning
To a new week:
Help us to live it for You.

We worship You, O God,
Lord and Master of our lives,
Our God, mighty in power,
Saving in Grace:
We come now as Your servants.

Help us, by our lives and witness,
so to commend You
That those we meet will see You working in us
And want to know You, too.

Amen.

❖ ❖ ❖ ❖ ❖

86. *Invocation*

God of storm and tempest,
Lord of the miraculous,
Grant us a vision of possibility
So compelling that we find it irresistible;
So vivid that we cannot disbelieve it;
So momentous that we cannot help but be influenced by it;
So all-embracing that we want to be enfolded in it,
Becalmed in You, through You, for You:
A glimpse of eternity
NOW

❖ ❖ ❖ ❖ ❖

87. *Act of Confession: The Open Book*

Lord God, You search us out,

You look deep into our hearts
and read the book of our lives;
You see pages that are dirty and dog-eared,
stained with carelessness,
spattered with the marks of our selfishness and greed.
Forgive us for those pages.

You look down from heaven
and see us in perspective,
You see us as little dots fused together into a picture,
some of us out of place,
not conforming to the pattern
because we think we know best.
Forgive us for our stubbornness.

You see the activities that engage us,
and the games we play with our lives.
You see our symbols and images,
the golden calves of materialism by which we betray You.
Forgive us for our denial of You.

Lord God, God of Love,
we stand convicted of these things,
of our lack of love and concern for others,
and most of all, of our lack of loyalty to You.

Forgive us, Lord, and heal us,
not because we deserve it,
but because it is Your Nature to love,
and we depend on it.

We thank You that You hear us,
that even as we say the words,
We know ourselves forgiven.

Amen

❖ ❖ ❖ ❖ ❖

88. A General Confession

We begin with a short time of quiet, conscious of our own needs and failings.

Father, we come to You in prayer, knowing our own limitations yet aware of the tremendous need around us. We ask Your forgiveness for our failures -
-   failure to speak Your Name to those who needed to hear it;
-   failure to show love and compassion;
-   failure in our relationships;
-   failure to put You and Your work first;
-   failure to give You priority in our lives;
-   failure in those areas of our personal lives, which we confess now in our hearts.

Hear and forgive us, we pray.

Father God, through Your Son You have promised that those who come to You in true repentance will be forgiven.

We claim that forgiveness, and praise You for it.

89. A General Intercession

As we think of the needs of others, the prayers we would see answered, let us first consider our own lives and witness and ask forgiveness for all those acts of thoughtlessness, selfishness and uncharitableness that may have turned others away from the Lord whom we profess to serve. We confess now.

Lord, have mercy on us and forgive us, we pray.

We remember now those who are victims of the inhumanity of others; those caught up in the senseless pursuit of war and power, especially in ....; those who are persecuted for their faith or their political principles.

Lord, have compassion on them, and grant them peace and freedom we pray.

We remember, too, those who wrong them by their greed,
selfishness and fear; those whose task is to lead, but who lead them only into fear, captivity and want.

Lord, have mercy on them and forgive them we pray.

We pray for all in positions of leadership and authority, in national and international politics, influential organisations, local and national government committees, especially.........

Lord, be present with them and guide them, we pray.

We remember those who are committed to the cause of peace............
those who seek to alleviate suffering and hardship in the world, and those who work in all areas of social concern, especially......
Lord, grant them strength and conviction, and guide them, we pray.

We remember those who are called to minister to others in the spreading of the Gospel and the advancement of the Faith, especially those known to us***.........
and in the work of the Bible Society in bringing the Word of God to people all over the world in their own language. Today we pray for their ministry in.....

Lord, lead those whom You call and grant them Your help and strength, we pray.

We think of all those who are in need of help and healing, especially those known to us ***....; those who are victims of natural disasters or events over which they had no control***....; for those who mourn the loss of loved ones***..... and for all those involved in the ministries of helping and healing and blessing in their lives.

We bring these prayers to You now, Lord, in the sure confidence that You will hear and answer, according to Your gracious will, through Jesus Christ our Lord.   Amen

***   **Please feel free to mention names silently or out loud.**

❖ ❖ ❖ ❖ ❖

90. Prayer of Dedication

Let us be still in the presence of the Lord.

Let us offer ourselves anew,
mind, body, heart and soul
to His Service,

through our service to His world,
open to the prompting
of His Loving Word,
willing to answer any call -
however great or small the task -
for He will be with us
Always

Amen

❖ ❖ ❖ ❖ ❖

91. An Offertory Prayer

Lord, as we bring to You these our gifts of money, we pray, too, that You will accept our whole selves, all that we have and are, to be used by You just as you will, and when, and where, to the greater glory of Your Kingdom here on earth.   Amen

92. Prayers of Intercession:
"In Trust and Confidence"

The Lord said to Joshua, *"Only be strong and very courageous..."*

(Joshua 1:7)

Faced with a turbulent world, where peace is such a rare commodity, where those countries which seem to be at peace still have strong undercurrents of opposition running through them, where innocent people live in fear and those who are misled live in hatred, to talk of courage and confidence seems out of place.

We pray for the many who live in such countries or communities, that they may be inspired to seek justice and live in peace with all people.

> V. Lord, we bring their needs to You.
> R. **Have compassion on them, we pray.**

God promised through His prophets, *"When you pass through the waters, I will be with You, and through the rivers, they shall not overwhelm you."*

(Isaiah 43:2)

We think of the many who are facing the storms of life at this time, whose confidence may be wavering, and for whom talk of trusting in God may seem unhelpful.

We pray for those in need of courage to face the future,
for whatever reason;
for those whose loved-ones are dying and those newly bereaved;
for those who struggle against social and cultural difficulties,
who are facing redundancy;
for those who are homeless and unemployed.
May they be enabled to find courage, and to live in dignity and peace.

> V. Lord, we bring their needs to You;
> R. **Make Your presence known to them, we pray.**

Paul told the sailors as they faced the storm, *"....none of you will lose a hair from your heads."* *(Acts 27:34b)*

We think of those who are sick and weak, close to despair, conscious of their own mortality;

of those in fear for their lives through persecution,
famine or natural disasters;
for those who have been institutionalised or handicapped and now have to
fend for themselves in a hostile environment;
those who are in prison, especially through no fault of their own;
for ex-offenders trying to make a new life yet always dogged by the past -
none of whom may have any concept of a God in whom they can trust.

We pray that they may be enabled to know the healing and supporting
Love of God through the love and friendship of His people.

> V. Lord, we bring their needs to You;
> R. **May Your healing love flood over them.**

Jesus told His frightened disciples, *"It is I; do not be afraid."*

(John 6:20)

We think of the Church at this time of uncertainty, where divisions threaten
yet talks of unity continue.

We pray for our President and Vice-President as they seek to be
ambassadors for the Methodist Church and for all those involved in the
serious decision-making about the future of the Church as an institution.
We pray that they may first seek God's will and not their own, and that
they may be enabled to act graciously when their personal hopes fail,
putting the good of the Kingdom of God before their own.

> V. Lord, we bring them to you;
> R. **May Your grace be sufficient for them at all times.**

And we pray for ourselves, here in this place, asking that we may be
enabled to witness and serve with greater trust and confidence, in and
through the Name of Jesus our Lord. Amen

MOORLEY'S

are growing Publishers, adding several new titles to our list each year. We also undertake private publications and commissioned works.

Our range of publications includes: **Books of Verse**
        Devotional Poetry
        Recitations
        Drama
        Bible Plays
        Sketches
        Nativity Plays
        Passiontide Plays
        Easter Plays
        Demonstrations
        Resource Books
        Assembly Material
        Songs & Musicals
        Children's Addresses
        Prayers & Graces
        Daily Readings
        Books for Speakers
        Activity Books
        Quizzes
        Puzzles
        Painting Books
        Daily Readings
        Church Stationery
        Notice Books
        Cradle Rolls
        Hymn Board Numbers

Please send a S.A.E. (approx 9" x 6") for the current catalogue or consult your local Christian Bookshop who should stock or be able to order our titles.